For my amazing team, I couldn't have done this without you!
Thanks for allowing me to write books for the kid I used to be;
you're literally letting me live my dream.

—B.R.

Tilbury House Publishers
Thomaston, Maine
www.tilburyhouse.com

First US edition 2023
ISBN: 978-1-958394-25-0

Original English language edition first published by Ladybird Books Ltd, 20 Vauxhall Bridge Road, London, SW1V 2SA, UK
Copyright © Ben Rothery, 2022
The moral right of the author/illustrator has been asserted. All rights reserved.

Printed in China
A CIP catalog record for this book is available from the British Library
ISBN: 978-0-241-53226-3

Measurements

You'll see a few metric measurements in this book. Metric measurements are used in most of the world, but a few countries (including the US) still use the Imperial system of inches, feet, ounces, and pounds. Here are some conversion formulas to get from one system to the other.

Length

To convert meters to feet, multiply by 3.281. To convert centimeters to inches, divide by 2.54.

- 1 meter (or metre) = 39.37 inches, or about 3 feet; 1 foot = 0.305 meter; 1 yard = 0.914 meter.
- 1 centimeter (or centimetre) = 0.39 inch, less than half an inch; 1 inch = 2.54 centimeters.
- 1 millimeter = 0.039 inch; 1 inch = 25.4 millimeters.
- 1 kilometer = 0.62 mile; 1 mile = 1.609 kilometers.

Weight/Mass

To convert grams to ounces, divide by 28.35. To convert kilograms to pounds, multiply by 2.205.

- 1 gram = 0.035 ounce; 1 ounce = 28.35 grams.
- 1 kilogram = 2.205 pounds; 1 pound = 0.454 kilogram; 1 ton = 2,000 pounds or 907 kilograms; 1 metric ton = 1,000 kilograms.

BEN ROTHERY'S

Deadly
AND
Dangerous
Animals

TILBURY HOUSE PUBLISHERS

Contents

 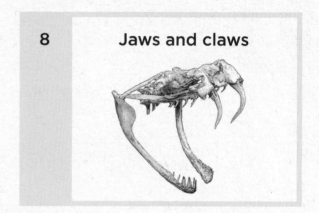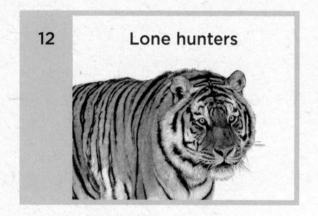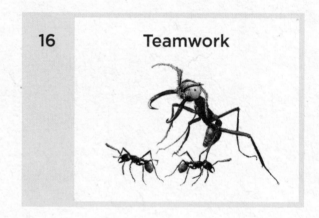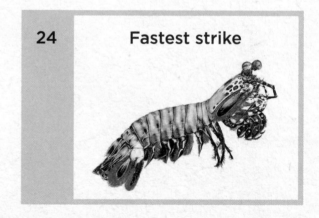

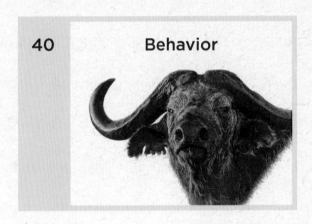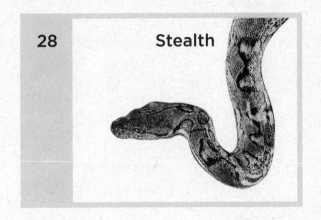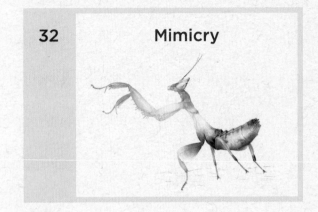

Introduction

When we think of deadly and dangerous animals, we often imagine the biggest hunters with the longest claws and the sharpest teeth. But there's much more to it than that.

Many different **species*** – from tiny ants to giant buffalo – use their speed, stealth and intelligence, as well as other special features, to find food, fight for **territory** and defend themselves.

From lightning speed to **poisonous** skin – and, yes, sharp teeth – let's explore what it takes to be counted among the deadliest animals on Earth . . .

*Definitions of words in **bold** can be found in the glossary on page 47.

7

Jaws and claws

Harpy eagle
Harpia harpyja

The South American harpy eagle has some of the longest claws on Earth – only the grizzly bear (*Ursus arctos horribilis*) has claws the same length! The eagle's huge talons, measuring up to 10 centimeters (4 inches) long, allow it to catch **prey** that weighs as much as it does.

Great white shark
Carcharodon carcharias

The jaws of a great white shark contain up to 300 **serrated** triangular teeth arranged in rows. Throughout the shark's life, new ones move forward to replace old ones that fall out or are damaged as the shark saws its food into chunks.

Goliath birdeater spider
Theraphosa blondi

The Goliath birdeater is the largest spider on Earth and has fangs to match. Each of its fangs is 5 centimeters (2 inches) long – that's almost as long as a front-door key. The spider uses these fangs like two needles to inject **venom** into its prey. The venom not only kills the spider's **victim** but also turns its insides into liquid, making it easier for the spider to eat.

Gaboon viper
Bitis gabonica

The Gaboon viper has the longest fangs of any snake species. Measuring up to 5 centimeters (2 inches) long, these fangs, along with very large venom glands, enable the viper to inject a huge quantity of venom with each bite. Its teeth also curve inwards, allowing it to bite and hold on to its prey tightly.

Saltwater crocodile
Crocodylus porosus

The saltwater crocodile is the world's largest **reptile**. It also has the strongest bite ever measured in a living animal, with a force of 25,500 kilopascals, or 3,698 pounds per square inch. (By comparison, a human has an average bite force of around 860 kilopascals, or 125 pounds per square inch.) This powerful bite is helped by a set of enormous muscles – the pterygoideus – located at the back of the crocodile's head.

Clouded leopard
Neofelis nebulosa

Location: Nepal to southern China

**Length: 130–199 centimeters
(51 to 78 inches)**

**Height: 50–55 centimeters
(20 to 22 inches)**

Weight: 11–23 kilograms (25 to 52 pounds)

When it comes to big cats, you could be forgiven for thinking that the biggest cat – the Siberian tiger – must have the biggest bite. But it's actually the clouded leopard, which is only one-eighth of the tiger's size, that claims that title.

A few features combine to make the clouded leopard's bite so deadly: **canines** measuring up to 9 centimeters (3.5 inches), a large gap called a diastema between the front and back teeth, and the ability to open its jaws to an angle of 100 degrees. As a result, the clouded leopard's bite is so powerful that it can crack through the back of its prey's skull – rather than using a bite to the throat to suffocate it, as most big cats do.

The back teeth of all cats are called **carnassials**. These teeth come in pairs of one upper tooth and one lower tooth. Their sharp edges pass by each other in a shearing manner – very similar to the blades on a pair of scissors – enabling the cat to cut meat from its prey. The cat then swallows these sliced-off chunks of meat whole.

incisors

carnassial teeth

diastema

canine teeth

Lone hunters

Animals that hunt other animals for food are called **carnivores**. Almost all carnivores live and hunt alone, including some of the most successful **predators** on Earth.

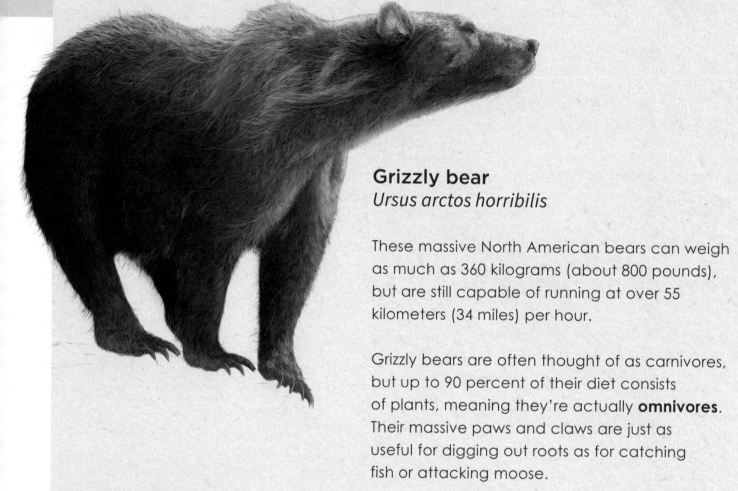

Grizzly bear
Ursus arctos horribilis

These massive North American bears can weigh as much as 360 kilograms (about 800 pounds), but are still capable of running at over 55 kilometers (34 miles) per hour.

Grizzly bears are often thought of as carnivores, but up to 90 percent of their diet consists of plants, meaning they're actually **omnivores**. Their massive paws and claws are just as useful for digging out roots as for catching fish or attacking moose.

Tasmanian devil
Sarcophilus harrisii

The Tasmanian devil is the world's largest carnivorous **marsupial**. Named after the island south of Australia that is its main home, it will eat almost anything, from insects to birds, and is capable of eating 40 percent of its own body weight in just half an hour. It even eats the flesh, hair, bones and teeth of its prey.

Black-footed cat
Felis nigripes

Weighing no more than 2 kilograms (4.5 pounds), one of the world's smallest cats is also the deadliest. The Southern African black-footed cat has a **hunting success rate** of 60 percent, while tigers, by comparison, are only successful 5–10 percent of the time. These little hunters catch up to fourteen small animals each night – that's more prey than a leopard captures in six months.

Siberian tiger
Panthera tigris altaica

The largest of the big cats is the Siberian tiger, which can weigh as much as 175 kilograms (almost 400 pounds). This massive cat will hunt anything – even other predators such as bears – by ambushing them from above, then killing them with a bite to the spine.

Lessert's rainbow spider
Stenaelurillus lesserti

This jumping spider possesses some of the best vision among **arthropods**.

There are over 6,000 species of jumping spiders, some of which can leap up to 50 times their own body length. They stalk to within leaping distance of their prey, pausing only to attach a safety line of silk before attacking.

Dragonfly
Anisoptera

Location: worldwide, except Antarctica
Length: 1.5–19.0 centimeters (0.6 to 7.5 inches)
Wingspan: 1.2–19.0 centimeters (0.5 to 7.5 inches)

Juvenile dragonflies, known as nymphs, are also greedy predators, and will eat almost any living thing smaller than they are.

Despite their small size, dragonflies are the deadliest hunters in the animal kingdom – probably because they've been doing it for a very, very long time: their ancestors first emerged around 300 million years ago.

There are 3,000 species of dragonflies, and adults catch up to 95 percent of the prey they chase, including bees, moths and even other dragonflies. No other species comes close to this remarkable success rate. When hunting, the dragonfly is aided by **specialized** eyes, which can pick up the dark shapes of other insects against the sky, and two pairs of wings, which are powered by individual muscles. These wings enable the dragonfly to move very easily and very quickly.

Teamwork

By working together, some animals are able to dramatically increase both how much prey they catch and how big that prey can be.

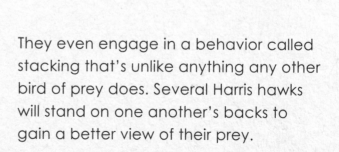

Harris hawk
Parabuteo unicinctus

With their keen eyesight, sharp beaks and powerful talons, Harris hawks are excellent hunters on their own, but these hawks prefer to hunt together. Each hawk takes up the role best suited to its abilities. The hawk with the best eyesight looks out for prey, while the faster ones chase the prey and make the kill, then all the hawks share their catch.

They even engage in a behavior called stacking that's unlike anything any other bird of prey does. Several Harris hawks will stand on one another's backs to gain a better view of their prey.

Spotted hyena
Crocuta crocuta

Spotted hyena live in groups of up to 80 individuals, known as clans. Unusually for **mammals**, females are the dominant leaders of these clans and are larger than the males.

Despite their reputation as scavengers that steal leftovers from lions and other predators, hyena are actually skilled hunters in their own right. They have large brains and use teamwork to bring down a range of prey, including antelope and wildebeest.

With their big skulls, specialized bone-crushing teeth and strong jaw muscles, hyena have an incredibly powerful bite. It's so powerful, in fact, that their skulls are reinforced to protect against the huge pressure from their jaws.

Burchell's army ant
Eciton burchellii

Working together as a single **colony** up to 200 meters long, Burchell's army ants can capture as many as 30,000 individual prey – including other ants and insects, frogs and lizards – in a single day.

African wild dog
Lycaon pictus

Location: Southern and Eastern Africa, but mainly Botswana, Namibia and Zimbabwe

Length: 100–153 centimeters (39 to 60 inches)

Height: 60–75 centimeters (24 to 30 inches)

Weight: 20–32 kilograms (45 to 72 pounds)

Despite their common English name, African wild dogs are not dogs at all, but the last living member of the *Lycaon* **genus**. Unlike dogs, they have special teeth that help them to shred meat, and they also lack a dewclaw – the claw some dogs have in much the same spot as a human thumb.

African wild dogs have strong jaws and powerful legs, and they hunt in teams. This allows them to hunt prey several times their size. Between 70 and 85 percent of their hunts end with a kill, compared to only 30 percent for the African lion.

These highly social animals are, like hyena, always led by a female. They care for their young together and vote for when to hunt by sneezing! The more sneezes from the gathered dogs, the more likely they are to hunt. They use endurance rather than strength to catch prey such as gazelle, sometimes chasing it over huge distances before working together to pull it down once it gets tired.

African wild dogs are fast eaters, but they also live alongside other predators like hyena, lions and leopards that will steal food if they can. So, for all their hunting skill, wild dogs still lose up to half of their kills to other large carnivores.

Sadly, African wild dogs are **endangered** due to being hunted by humans and the loss of their habitat. There are only around 5,000 left in the wild.

Speed

When it comes to deadliness, one of a hunter's most useful skills is how quickly it can move.

Cheetah
Acinonyx jubatus

Cheetahs are the fastest animals on land, having been recorded running at speeds of up to 96 kilometers (60 miles) per hour. But it's the ease with which they can change direction that makes them even more deadly.

Cheetahs have very good eyesight, and their coats are **camouflaged** to blend in with their surroundings. Moving stealthily, they creep up close to their prey before unleashing their devastating speed.

Cheetahs are able to reach their full speed in only three seconds and, using their long tails for balance, they can turn quicker than any other land-based predator. This gives them a hunting success rate of almost 60 percent.

Golden eagle
Aquila chrysaetos

Golden eagles have a huge wingspan of around 2 meters and are the second-fastest animal on Earth. Their long, broad wings and outstretched feathers enable them to fly quickly and to glide effortlessly. They cruise at around 50 kilometers (30 miles) per hour, but can reach up to 320 kilometers (200 miles) per hour when attacking their prey.

Shortfin mako
Isurus oxyrinchus

Capable of reaching speeds of up to 74 kilometers (46 miles) per hour, the shortfin mako is the speediest shark and one of the fastest fish on the planet.

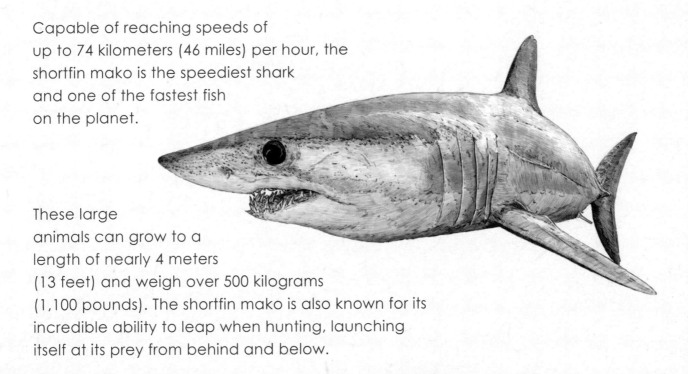

These large animals can grow to a length of nearly 4 meters (13 feet) and weigh over 500 kilograms (1,100 pounds). The shortfin mako is also known for its incredible ability to leap when hunting, launching itself at its prey from behind and below.

Peregrine falcon
Falco peregrinus

Location: worldwide, except for Antarctica and New Zealand
Length: 34–58 centimeters (13 to 23 inches)
Wingspan: 74–120 centimeters (29 to 47 inches)

The peregrine falcon is not just the fastest bird of prey but the quickest living animal. It's superbly built to hunt at speed, with an **aerodynamic** shape, sharply pointed wings and stiff feathers.

This impressive hunter feeds on other birds and bats, which it catches in flight. First, it soars to a great height above its prey, then it dives steeply, reaching speeds of up to 389 kilometers (241 miles) per hour. It strikes its target with its foot clenched like a fist, aiming at one wing to avoid hurting itself. The speed and force of this impact stuns or kills the prey, which the falcon then turns to catch in midair before carrying it off to eat.

Fastest strike

It's not just how swiftly an animal can move that makes it deadly, but also how quickly it can strike.

Secretary bird
Sagittarius serpentarius

This large African bird of prey has long legs like a stork. It patrols the plains south of the Sahara Desert, from Senegal in the west to Somalia in the east, hunting and catching its prey on the ground.

The secretary bird can kick with a force equal to five times its own body weight and a contact time of less than 15 milliseconds. Its ability to target the exact location of its prey's head before striking – a vital feature for an animal whose diet includes venomous snakes and scorpions – suggests that it has excellent eyesight.

Trapdoor ant
Odontomachus brunneus

This ant has the fastest strike
in the world and is capable
of closing its jaws extremely
quickly. But it doesn't use its
mouth simply to attack its prey –
it also uses it like a slingshot
to hurl **intruders** out of its nest
or to throw itself backwards
to escape a threat.

Peacock mantis shrimp
Odontodactylus scyllarus

This aggressive **crustacean** possesses
one of the fastest limb movements
in the animal kingdom. The shrimp's
punch is so fast that it causes the
water in front of it to boil as its
fist-like club passes through.

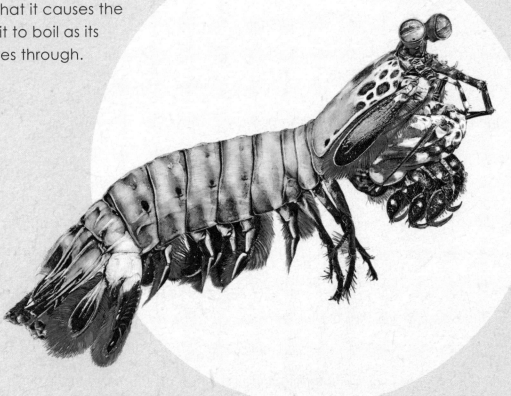

Chameleon
Chamaeleonidae

Location: Africa (including Madagascar), southern Europe, southern Asia
Length: 2–68 centimeters (0.8 to 27 inches)
Weight: 0.1–2.0 kilograms (0.2 to 4.5 pounds)

With their incredible color-changing abilities and nearly 360-degree vision, chameleons are already excellent hunters, but surprisingly it's their tongues that make them really deadly.

Once a chameleon has locked eyes on its prey – such as an ant or other insect – it fires its tongue towards its intended meal at over 2.2 kilometers (1.4 miles) per second and as far as two and a half times the length of its own body.

Chameleons also produce a sticky **mucus** on the tips of their tongues. This mucus is 400 times thicker than human saliva, meaning that anything caught in it is very unlikely to escape.

Stealth

Some animals use stealth to either approach their prey unseen or wait for it to come to them before unleashing their attack.

Sargassum fish
Histrio histrio

The sargassum fish spends its life hiding among clumps of sargassum seaweed, which floats in subtropical oceans. An ambush hunter, this fish uses its special fins to grasp and climb through the seaweed. Once in position, it stays still, relying on its spotted camouflage to remain hidden until the last moment.

When it strikes, the sargassum fish rapidly expands its mouth to many times its original size, drawing prey into its mouth with the suction created by the strike. This also enables it to swallow creatures larger than itself.

Northern pike
Esox lucius

This large freshwater fish remains stationary in the water, waiting until its prey moves into range. Before striking, the pike bends its torpedo-shaped body almost into an S shape, then lunges forward using its powerful tail and fins.

Once a pike latches on to its food, it rarely lets go. Its jaws are lined with long, fanged teeth, and it has as many as 700 smaller backwards-facing teeth lining the roof of its mouth.

Snow leopard
Panthera uncia

These ambush hunters use the low light of dawn and dusk to stalk prey that is sometimes up to three times their own weight.

Using their camouflaged fur, snow leopards hide among the rocks and snow of their mountain homes, and prefer to attack from above, jumping up to 15 meters (49 feet) to surprise their prey.

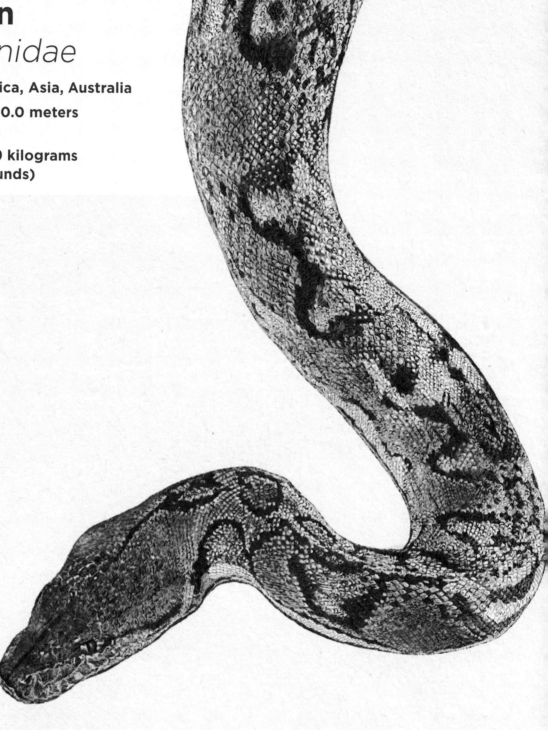

Python
Pythonidae

Location: Africa, Asia, Australia

**Length: 0.6–10.0 meters
(2 to 33 feet)**

**Weight: 1–159 kilograms
(2 to 350 pounds)**

The python family of non-venomous snakes includes 42 species, some of which are the largest snakes in the world. Native to Southeast Asia, the reticulated python (*Malayopython reticulatus*) is the world's longest snake and one of the heaviest: the largest ever recorded was caught in 1912 and measured an incredible 10 meters long.

Pythons have weak eyesight, but the strong chemical sensors in their tongues and heat sensors along their jaws help them to detect their prey. They hide in a camouflaged position until their prey – such as a bird or a monkey – comes close enough to strike using their sharp backwards-curving teeth.

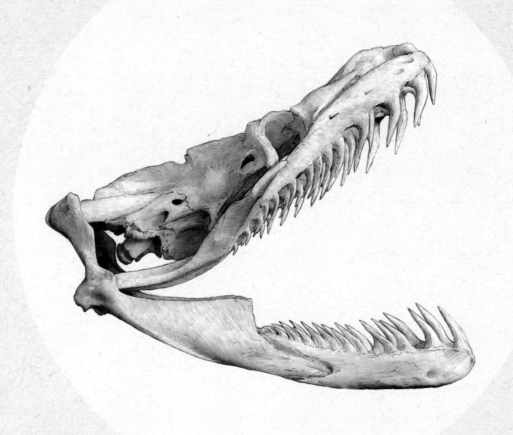

After the python has latched on, it quickly wraps around the animal, squeezing out the air until it dies. Then the python eats its prey whole. Since the bones in its skull are not fixed together, it can move its skull and jaws along the prey to swallow it.

Mimicry

Some animals behave, look or sound a lot like other animals in order to trick their prey into coming closer so they can catch them. This is called **mimicry**.

Alligator snapping turtle
Macrochelys temminckii

Weighing as much as 113 kilograms (250 pounds), the alligator snapping turtle is among the largest freshwater turtles in the world. With its spiked shell and beaklike jaws, it has no natural predators and can stay underwater for up to 50 minutes before surfacing for air.

The alligator snapping turtle's tongue has a red piece of flesh at the tip that looks like a worm. The turtle waves this around to attract fish or frogs while lying in wait on the riverbed. When its prey gets close enough, the turtle lunges forward and snaps its jaws shut.

Assassin bug
Stenolemus bituberus

This crafty bug catches its preferred prey – spiders – using a behavior known as aggressive mimicry. First, it plucks at the silk threads of a spiderweb in a way that creates the same vibrations as a small insect struggling to escape. This fools the spider into heading towards the bug. Once the spider is within reach, the assassin bug stabs its prey with its sharp snout.

Margay
Leopardus wiedii

Nicknamed "the monkey cat," the margay spends most of its life high in the treetops of Central America. Superbly camouflaged and with sharp claws and teeth, this hunter can leap up to 4 meters (13 feet) from tree to tree.

But it's the margay's use of mimicry that makes it truly deadly. Margays have been observed copying the calls of the baby pied tamarin (*Saguinus bicolor*) in order to lure the squirrel-sized adult tamarins closer, making them easier to catch.

Orchid mantis
Hymenopus coronatus

Location: Southeast Asia
Length: 3–6 centimeters (1.2 to 2.4 inches)

A species of praying mantis, the orchid mantis employs two very different strategies to catch its prey.

The smaller male mantis camouflages himself to hide within an orchid, the flower from which these mantises get their name. Hidden, he lies in wait until his prey gets close enough to catch.

The much larger female doesn't hide in an orchid, however. She pretends to be one. The pollinating insects like bees that she feeds on are attracted to a flower's shape and brightness, and she uses this to her advantage.

The mantis twists herself into a perfect orchid shape and displays brighter colors than any natural orchid could achieve.

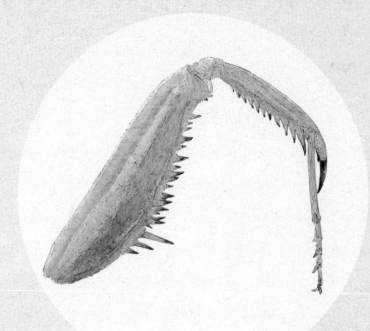

When her prey gets close enough, the mantis lashes out with one of the fastest strikes in nature, impaling the insect on spiked limbs before biting off its head and eating it.

Venom and poison

The word "venomous" is used to describe creatures that inject toxins – a type of **poison** – into other animals to defend themselves or to disable their prey, or to do both. For example, snakes and spiders harm other animals using fangs, stings, spines or saliva.

The word "poisonous" is used to describe creatures that use toxins only as a defensive weapon – unloading but not injecting the toxins when attacked or eaten. For example, certain frogs deliver toxins through their skin when another creature touches or tries to eat them.

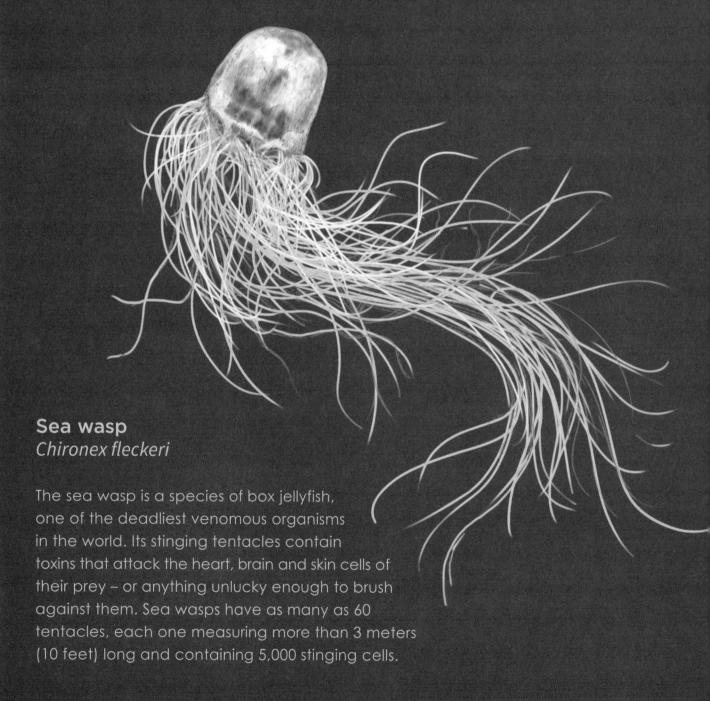

Sea wasp
Chironex fleckeri

The sea wasp is a species of box jellyfish, one of the deadliest venomous organisms in the world. Its stinging tentacles contain toxins that attack the heart, brain and skin cells of their prey – or anything unlucky enough to brush against them. Sea wasps have as many as 60 tentacles, each one measuring more than 3 meters (10 feet) long and containing 5,000 stinging cells.

Pufferfish
Tetraodontidae

Since they are slow-moving and clumsy, pufferfish have developed a number of features to defend themselves from predators. When threatened, the pufferfish doesn't try to swim away. Instead, it quickly swallows huge amounts of water, puffing up to several times its original size and becoming a giant ball that can't be eaten. This is where it gets its name from, but it's another feature that makes it deadly.

Almost all pufferfish contain tetrodotoxin, a poisonous substance they absorb from their food. This poison makes them taste bad and is often deadly to predators, so many species of animals warn of this danger through their bright colors and patterns. Tetrodotoxin is deadly to humans – there is enough in one pufferfish to kill 30 humans, and there is no known antidote.

Golden poison frog
Phyllobates terribilis

The brightly colored golden poison frog is one of the most toxic animals on Earth. A single frog measuring just 5 centimeters (2 inches) long contains enough poison to kill several adult humans.

This tiny frog doesn't make its own poison, though. Instead, it collects poison from the tiny beetles it eats, then releases it through glands on its skin to protect itself from potential predators.

Inland taipan
Oxyuranus microlepidotus

Australia's inland taipan is the world's most venomous snake, with the most toxic poison of any reptile. Its deadly venom contains a mix of different toxins that kill rapidly by attacking the muscles, blood and brain of the snake's prey.

The taipan's ability to kill its prey quickly prevents the small mammals it hunts from escaping or potentially harming it.

Boomslang
Dispholidus typus

This species of large tree
snake from Southern Africa
is able to open its jaws to an
angle of 170 degrees. This wide
bite enables the boomslang
to use the large fangs at the back of its jaw to
deliver its strong venom, which contains a chemical that
affects its prey's blood, making the boomslang very deadly.

Boomslangs are shy snakes and, when not hunting,
only attack if they're threatened.

Behavior

Some species are especially deadly not just because of their physical features, but also their bad-tempered or fearless behavior.

Black mamba
Dendroaspis polylepis

The black mamba is the largest venomous snake in Africa and one of the fastest snakes on Earth, but what makes it really deadly is its aggressive personality when cornered.

Mambas are shy and will try to escape when threatened, but if they can't get away they will defend themselves against animals many times larger than they are. Lifting the first third of their bodies off the ground, black mambas strike repeatedly, injecting large amounts of deadly venom into their targets.

Honey badger
Mellivora capensis

Although honey badgers usually hunt for their own food, they will happily steal from other animals or scavenge the kills of larger carnivores. They will eat almost anything, from insects and reptiles to birds and small mammals, as well as roots, fruits and, yes, honey.

Despite weighing no more than 16 kilograms (36 pounds), honey badgers are fearless. They will fight back against – and even chase off – much larger predators, including lions and leopards.

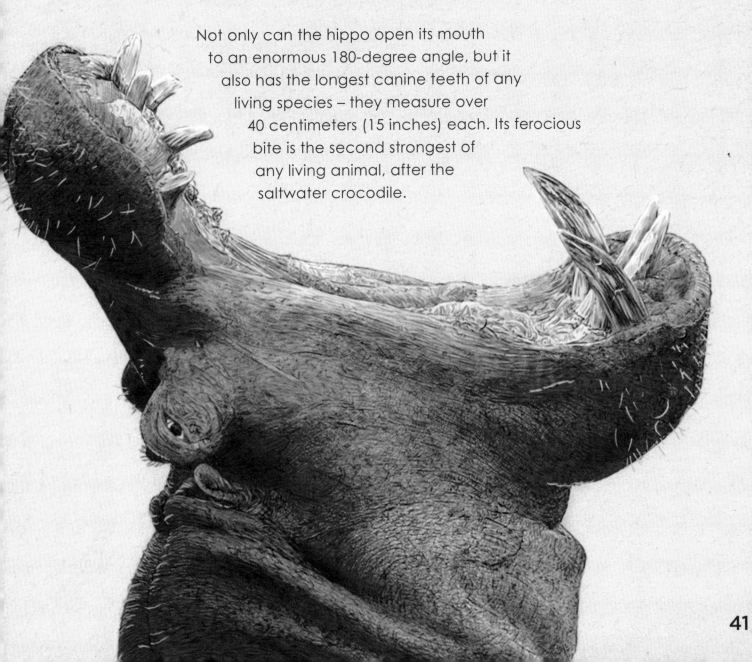

Hippopotamus
Hippopotamus amphibious

The hippopotamus is the world's deadliest **semi-aquatic** mammal.

Hippos might look slow and gentle, but these **territorial** and aggressive animals are able to move at speeds of up to 48 kilometers (30 miles) per hour on land. They live in herds of between 10 and 20 individuals, and will attack other animals that get too close to them. Hippos also kill an estimated 500 people a year on the African continent.

Not only can the hippo open its mouth to an enormous 180-degree angle, but it also has the longest canine teeth of any living species – they measure over 40 centimeters (15 inches) each. Its ferocious bite is the second strongest of any living animal, after the saltwater crocodile.

Cape buffalo
Syncerus caffer

Location: Southern and Eastern Africa
Length: 3.4 meters (11 feet)
Height: 1.7 meters (5.6 feet)
Weight: 1,000 kilograms (2,200 pounds)

The Cape buffalo is known
as one of the most dangerous
African animals. It weighs as
much as 1,000 kilograms, is able to
run at speeds of nearly 60 kilometers
(37 miles) per hour and has sharp, curved
horns, meaning it can easily defend itself.
But the thing that earns it the nickname
"black death" is its bad temper.

Although Cape buffalo will generally try to escape
from a threat, once angered they actively
hunt their attackers. The buffalo circle their enemies –
even lions – before attempting to either kill the predators
with their horns or trample them with their hooves.

Deadliest to humans

Although sharks, snakes and spiders have fearsome reputations, none of them is the deadliest animal to humans. Nor are crocodiles, bears or any of the large land mammals we share this planet with. The deadliest species to humans is actually something much smaller: the mosquito.

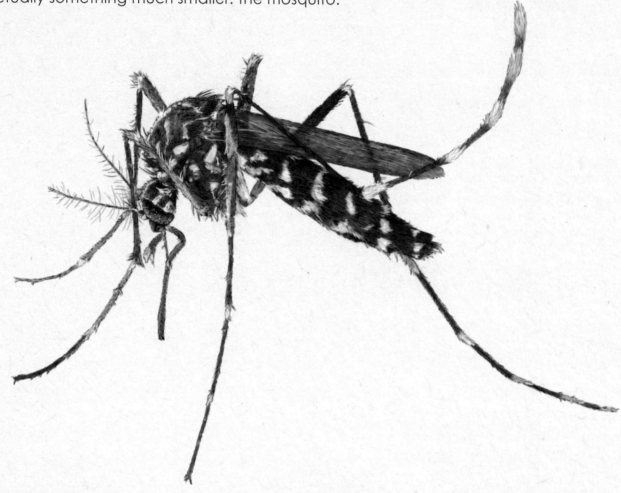

Marsh mosquito
Anopheles

Location: worldwide, except for Antarctica and Iceland

Length: 1.2–2.5 centimeters (0.5 to 1 inch)

Across the globe, snakes are responsible for up to 138,000 human deaths a year. Sharks kill fewer than 20 people. More than 400,000 people, however, die from **malaria**, which is a disease carried by mosquitoes.

It's the sheer number of mosquitoes and their wide distribution that make them so dangerous. Mosquitoes can be found in almost every part of the world, at various times of year, and in breeding season they outnumber every animal on Earth except ants and termites.

It is the female mosquito that bites, as she requires blood to produce her eggs. Males are harmless and feed only on flower nectar.

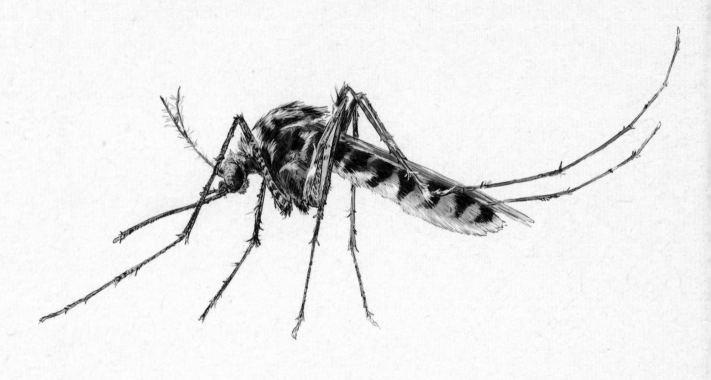

The female's mouthparts work like a needle to pierce the skin and enable her to suck out blood. She has special saliva that lines this opening in the victim's skin, allowing the blood to flow better.

Unfortunately for humans, this is where deadly blood-borne diseases are transmitted. As the mosquito bites person after person, her special saliva may also contain traces of any deadly diseases a previous victim may have been carrying, which she then passes on as she feeds. This means any infections can spread rapidly among a human population.

Dear reader,

In these pages we've met some incredible species with features that make them deadly or dangerous in the animal kingdom. But we've left the deadliest until last: humans.

With more than 7 billion people on the planet, we are the most numerous large animal. True, we lack strong bites and harmful venom, but what makes humans different is our brains, which we use to adapt quickly to many different situations.

This means humans live for a long time and take up a lot of space, which makes a big difference to our planet. Our behavior has caused the loss of habitats. We've hunted and fished many species to the edge of extinction, and we've accelerated global warming. If this continues, scientists predict that up to half of all species on Earth will face extinction in less than 80 years. Once they're gone, they're gone forever.

Luckily, our intelligence can also be our most positive feature if we use it to look after our planet and the animals we share it with. That includes doing things like reducing, reusing and recycling our belongings; walking or cycling as much as possible; eating more plant-based food and protecting the world's natural habitats.

Together, we can reduce the human impact on our planet to ensure the survival of all these amazing animals.

Ben

Glossary

aerodynamic
a description of an animal or object whose shape lets it glide or fly easily

arthropod
an animal without a backbone and with a hard covering

camouflage
When animals are colored or patterned to match their surroundings. This helps them to hide from *predators*.

canine tooth/canines
the pointed teeth that *mammals* have, which look a bit like fangs

carnassial tooth/carnassials
Meat-eating animals like dogs, bears and cats have big, sharp triangular teeth called *carnassials* at the back of their mouths.

carnivore
an animal that eats only other animals

colony
a group of animals of one kind that all live together

crustacean
an *arthropod* that mostly lives in the water

endangered
Animals that are at risk of disappearing from Earth forever. When the last animal in an *endangered species* dies, that *species* becomes extinct.

genus
species of animals or plants that are closely related to each other

hunting success rate
a number that tells us how many times out of 100 a *predator* catches and kills its *prey*

intruder
an animal that comes into another animal's space or *territory*

malaria
a serious disease that mosquitoes carry and spread to humans by drinking blood

mammal
A warm-blooded animal that breathes air, has a backbone, and grows hair or fur. Female *mammals* make milk to feed their young.

marsupial
a *mammal* that carries its babies around in a pouch

mimicry
When a creature or plant looks a lot like another living thing. This may mean they don't get eaten, or it can help them to get food.

mucus
a thick and slimy liquid that is produced in certain parts of an animal's body

omnivore
A *mammal* that eats both animals and plants. When an animal is an *omnivore*, we say that it is "omnivorous."

poison
something that causes harm when it enters an animal's body or touches its skin

poisonous
a description of an animal that contains a *poison*, and which may therefore harm another animal if touched or eaten by it

predator
an animal that hunts other animals

prey
an animal that is hunted, killed and eaten by another animal

reptile
a cold-blooded animal that breathes air, has a backbone and has scales instead of fur or feathers

semi-aquatic
an animal that lives some of the time on land and some of the time in water

serrated
something that has a sharp, jagged edge

specialized
Body parts that are adapted to perform certain tasks are known as *specialized* features.

species
a group of animals or plants that are the same or very similar, and can breed with each other to produce young

territorial
A creature or *species* that defends its *territory* from *intruders* is acting in a *territorial* way.

territory
the space an animal uses for feeding, breeding or raising its young

venom
a type of *poison* injected into other creatures by biting or stinging

victim
A creature that is hurt or killed by another. See also *prey*.

Ben Rothery is a detail-obsessed illustrator from Norwich, England, via Cape Town. He combines multiple processes to create intricate and delicate illustrations and repeating patterns, full of fine detail and vibrant color.

Much of Ben's work is inspired or informed by his love of nature – he grew up wanting variously to be a shark, a dinosaur or David Attenborough crossed with Indiana Jones, but settled on illustration as a way to bring those fantasies to life on paper.

Ben works from a small studio in London, which he shares with an unnecessarily large collection of very sharp pencils.